SELLING POWER'S BEST

123

SUPER SALES
TIPS

The best sales action tips by readers of
Selling Power magazine

compiled by the editors of *Selling Power*

123

SUPER SALES TIPS

The best sales action tips by readers of
Selling Power magazine

compiled by the editors of *Selling Power*

Selling Power's Best: 123 Super Sales Tips is published in the
United States by Personal Selling Power Inc.,
P.O. Box 5467, Fredericksburg, VA 22403
Tel. 540/752-7000
http://www.sellingpower.com

Book and Jacket designed by Jennifer D. Linch

Library of Congress Catalog Card# 97-76459

ISBN# 0-939613-14-X

Acknowledgements

From the many real-life sales stories published in *Selling Power* as Reader To Reader Tips, the editors have selected 123 of the very best for this book. In addition to the tips themselves, we have added quotes from the famous and not so famous – people who have something of value to share with sales professionals.

The editors wish to express their thanks to all the sales professionals who, over the years, have contributed their insights, expertise and stories of selling experiences to *Selling Power*. They have given readers a rich and powerful history of the real world of selling.

What you will get
from this book

The selling tips in this book come directly from the field and straight from the heart. The *Selling Power* readers who have written them learned valuable lessons that shaped their selling careers. Such stories are all one of a kind. Shared with others, they form a core of real world data that all sales professionals can use to expand their sales expertise. By trying these tips, or modifying them for individual sales calls, salespeople can stock a huge storehouse of creativity to draw from when the situation demands it. Reading stories and learning from peers can help you do better on your next sales call. With constant improvement comes more confidence and more successful selling. By reading the selling lessons in this book, you can practice continual improvement on a regular basis.

Stories are one of the oldest ways of relating information and transferring experience. This book follows a time-tested tradition of storytelling and story selling. The power in these pages can unlock more sales in your future. Read them for entertainment. Read them for pleasure.

Read them for the lessons. Read them for information. Then sit down and write out your own selling tips. Share them with other salespeople. By teaching, we learn. By learning, we grow. By growing, everybody wins.

To share a Selling Tip with *Selling Power* readers, type it out (no more than one page, double spaced) and mail it to: Selling Power, P.O. Box 5467, Fredericksburg, VA 22403. If we publish it, you'll receive $100.

How to use this book

To get the most out of this book of real-life sales tips, think about the sales in your own career. What were the basic lessons you learned? When did you first start to feel confident? What sale taught you the most valuable lesson? Are you still growing as a professional? What areas need the most work? What plan do you have for self-improvement? Such questions and others should raise your level of awareness and spur you on to greater growth and better selling techniques.

To use these tips to sell with more confidence, study the basic elements of each one. Jot down what made the tip work and how you could use the same technique or skill to close your next sale or series of sales. Clip these notes to the pages of the tips that are particularly helpful to you and refer back to them over the next weeks and months.

Keep this book with you. After a call that went well, jot down a few notes on what you think went right, what you could have done better, what you learned. Don't be judgmental. Simply record events and impressions. If a sale went badly, do the same thing. Try to analyze what went wrong then make a note of what you would do differently the next time you're in a similar situation.

Start to keep a log of your most memorable sales. Remember your past successes and failures and add to them your current sales experiences. Share them with other professionals and soon you will have a valuable asset in your own sales wisdom. Use these sales lessons to train new salespeople, to improve, by small increments, your own sales closing ratio and to reduce the stress that comes from repeating the same mistakes over and over. By following these guidelines, you can use these *Super Sales Tips* to help your sales grow.

I saw the sign

I sell signs – a high-visibility item, and almost every business needs one! Whenever I close a sale, I jot down the names of businesses adjacent to my new customer. Then later, after we've installed the sign, I send a postcard announcing the sign's arrival to those businesses on my list. Of course, I include information on how they, too, can get a great sign like my customer's. Response is terrific! Every time prospects pass our sign, they're reminded of my products, and the postcard tells them exactly where they can get them. This idea works well for those who sell any products used or displayed in the public eye: aluminum siding, painting services, paving work, brick and stone work, roofing, lawn and landscaping services – the possibilities are endless.

Jane Connor, Salesperson/Owner

> **"Doing business without advertising is like winking at a girl in the dark. You know what you are doing, but nobody else does."**
>
> **STEUART HENDERSON BRITT**

Information please

When you fulfill a request for product information, remind your prospects why they called or wrote for more information. If your prospects have too much on their minds to remember their request and what prompted them to make it, your literature may end up in the garbage with other unsolicited material. If a specific ad or product feature grabbed your prospect's attention, your response should take advantage of it. Instead of sending a deluge of information on your entire product line, customize literature packages with information on products or features in which the prospect took a special interest. A more personalized approach to information distribution may bring you more interested prospects and greater sales.

Ralph Pehrson, Sales Professional

Money well spent

As an advertising salesperson with the Gannett Rochester newspaper, I always closed my presentations to new prospects with, "I'll spend your money like it's my own." My words often helped reassure clients who were unfamiliar with costs, coverage, rates and other factors that determine the price and benefits of advertising. In most cases the prospect appreciated my concern and responded, "I think that's fair, and I'm going along with your suggestions."

Lester Edelman, Advertising-New Business

> **"Give them quality. That's the best kind of advertising."**
>
> **MILTON S. HERSHEY**

> **"True luck consists not in holding the best of the cards at the table: / Luckiest he who knows just when to rise and go home."**
>
> JOHN HAY

Cut the deck

I sell playing cards and I conduct a lot of business through trade shows. Prior to a show, I will send a memo to contacts and clients indicating what items are in the show and including five super-jumbo playing cards. In the letter, I state that they should bring the cards to my booth and we will "cut the deck." If any of their cards match the cut deck, they will receive a prize. This has proven to be very successful so far, and it entices more people to come over to my booth.

Amy Bruno, Area Manager

Parking lot presentation

Most salespeople can always use one more creative way to get an audience with their prospects. Here's mine: After hearing for the zillionth time that a prospect doesn't have the time to see me I respond, "Fine, then I'll meet you in your company parking lot. What time do you arrive at work?" The answer often throws my prospects off guard, so I explain that I've visited the prospect's office building several times and know that it takes at least three minutes to walk from the parking lot to the building elevators. I then say, "If I'm willing to meet you in the parking lot when you arrive at work, would you allow me to walk you to the building and talk to you for those three minutes?" One of my prospects asked me if I was serious, then offered me 15 minutes with him in his office the next day at the time I specified. When all else fails, this technique may get you that ever-elusive appointment.

Robert M. Peterson, Doctoral Student,
former Printing Salesperson

Organized gratitude

My salespeople send thank-you cards to more than 250 advertising clients who run ads in our weekly national trade publication. To simplify the process I drew up a simple "log sheet" for my salespeople that keeps track of their new clients. As they bring in new advertisers throughout the week, they take down such pertinent information as account numbers and contact names. Then, during down time they can look up each client in their computer database and send the thank-you note with a personal message and business card. The thank-you notes help increase repeat business and strengthen the client-salesperson relationship.

Carrie Anderson, Manager

> **"A thankful heart is the parent of all virtues."**
>
> **CICERO**

Sometimes I say no

My company manufactures an application-dependent high-tech product used by petrochemical companies, manufacturing facilities and municipalities to measure levels in process vessels. Specifying this type of product requires a thorough knowledge of the customer's expectations, the application specifics and the correct product. In many cases our product is not the best solution to the customer's requirement, even though it may work. In cases like this I prefer to suggest the best alternative even if it's not my product. This approach of saying, "No, I think there is a better alternative than my product for this specific application" has built up trust and confidence with my customers. I may not make that sale, but that person spreads the word all over the plant and to his friends in other industries. This source of referrals builds a strong and loyal customer base that keeps on expanding. This customer base is also more value conscious and appreciative.

Don Nahrstedt, Vice President

Postcards from the show

At trade shows where you meet lots of people and hold many meetings, try this great technique that has been successful for me. I get postcards from the city we are in and send the client/prospect a short note on the card saying, "Glad we saw each other, will follow up with the proposal, etc., next week." They see the postcard in their mail when they return from the trip and it definitely makes you stand out from the crowd. It also reminds them of the meeting you had at the show.

Andrea Nierenberg, Sales Professional

"All letters, methinks, should be as free and easy as one's discourse, not studied as an oration, nor made up of hard words like a charm."

DOROTHY OSBORNE

Stamp of approval

Several years ago, as administrative assistant in the marketing department of a company that manufactures and sells equipment to radio stations, I was given the task of researching the Canadian market. We wanted to find out what stations would be replacing old equipment, when, and what products were favored. We also wanted to know what new technology was needed by the industry. I had to make sure we received good, reliable information. After pondering the best way to get the most returns, I hit upon the idea of using a Canadian postage stamp on the self-addressed return envelopes. I acquired the stamps through a very good customer in Canada and mailed a survey form to 295 Canadian radio stations, addressed to the attention of the station engineer. I expected a good return, but was astonished when 105 completed forms came back. It was evident the use of the Canadian postage stamp had accomplished a remarkable 35 percent return. During the following year, as a result of the information obtained from the survey, our sales team was able

to increase equipment sales in Canada.

Nelda Hendon, Manager, Domestic Broadcast Sales

"Research is to see what everybody has seen, and to think what nobody else has thought."

ALBERT SZENT-GYORGYI

Faxed impressions

Here's an easy way to establish familiarity with prospects before your initial contact: Make a list of 10 potential customers. Next, use the decision maker's title to ask the receptionist for that person's first and last name and personal fax number. Tell the receptionist you understand that time is money and that you'd like to fax information about your product or service so that the decision maker can read about it and call if interested. Write a brief, warm, personal cover letter that tells the decision maker you'll be calling soon to follow up, and fax it to the decision maker with your product literature. In three to four days, call the decision maker, introduce yourself and make sure the fax arrived safely. Your fax should help heat up an otherwise cold call.

Rita Peters, Sales Professional

Turn your prospect upside-down

We can all use one more way to get an elusive prospect's attention. Use

this technique to show your prospects that your approach is truly

unique. Instead of sending the traditional business

letter, type your letter upside-down on your compa-

ny letterhead. The idea may seem a little crazy, but

it works. It gets the prospect's attention: Some sim-

ply want to know what kind of person types letters

upside-down; others feel that because your approach

is unusual, you will be creative in problem solving.

Woody Galyean, District Sales Representative

> **"It's terrible to allow convention-al habits to gain a hold on a whole household..."**
>
> **ZELDA FITZGERALD**

> **"America is becoming a nation of risk-takers, and the way we do business will never be the same."**
>
> **ALLAN KENNEDY**

Take a chance on me

Need an easy, inexpensive way to get a response from a hard-to-reach prospect? Send a lottery ticket with a short note that reads, "I'm giving you a chance with the lottery – how about giving me a chance?" That one little ticket not only gets my prospect's attention – it usually gets me an appointment.

Debbie Atchison, Sales Consultant

Survey your territory

As a new salesperson taking over a lot of "dead" accounts, I needed a way to introduce myself to my customers, find out more about them and recapture their business. I found the solution in a survey. I mailed surveys to all my contacts, introducing myself and explaining that I wanted to play a larger role in their success. I asked questions that would allow me to recommend products to save them money. After a few months, I sent a second survey titled "Do you ever wish you could have things just the way you want them? Now you can!" The survey contained a variety of questions: Are you the contact person? What are the best times to reach you? Do I contact you too often/not often enough? Are you familiar with our complete product line? You might be surprised at the large number of responses you receive and how effectively the survey can build rapport and sales.

Cara Anderson, Sales Consultant

Humor by fax

The Dale Carnegie courses I've attended often emphasize the value of humor in the workplace. To keep my customers smiling I keep a file of jokes to fax to them when the need arises. Amusing cover sheets, for example, help make my requests for credit applications a more pleasant experience. Over the years, many of my customers have returned the favor and faxed me humorous jokes and stories of their own, which builds rapport and keeps my own file growing. When your customers can count on getting a laugh out of your faxes, they'll look forward to hearing from you.

Laurie Jones, Account Executive

> **"Good humor makes all things tolerable."**
>
> **HENRY WARD BEECHER**

> **"To know when one's self is interested, is the first condition of interesting other people."**
>
> **WALTER PATER**

Shoestring selling

I always send out an introductory letter to warm up my cold calls, but I want my letters to stand out from every other salesperson's. In each one I enclose a shoestring and open my letter with, "Buying (type of product I sell) is about as exciting as buying shoelaces. Let me change all that for you." When I call to set up an appointment my prospects know exactly who I am, and my response is much better than the response to a regular old cold call.

Terri Job, Sales Consultant

Introducing... your sales staff

As a sales manager for a temporary help company, I spend a lot of time on the road visiting prospects and customers. Customers often come in to place orders when I'm away from the office. When they do, they have to trust people they've never met to serve their needs, and I have to trust my staff to make a great first impression in my absence. Since I can't take my team around and introduce them to all my customers, I do the next best thing. Instead of distributing a fancy brochure describing my company I have one that highlights my team's experience and special talents. Customers love learning a little about the people they might speak with when they call or come in. One new customer even went to the same college and majored in the same field as one of my staff members, which helped create instant rapport. When your customers are comfortable with the entire sales staff, trust and rapport automatically increase.

Nancy Hahn, Sales and Marketing Manager

The "Friday Fax"

To remind field salespeople of current promotions, new product intro-

ductions, price changes, new personnel or any other relevant infor-

mation, my company sends a "Friday Fax" each week. At the end of

every Thursday we fax a one-page notice to all our outside represen-

tatives that opens with a friendly greeting and closes with an inspir-

ing quote. The "Friday Fax" is a creative, upbeat way

to let your field salespeople know you haven't for-

gotten about them and to keep them informed in an

appealing way.

Larry Easterlin, Vice President of
Sales and Marketing

> **"Kindness effects**
> **more than**
> **severity."**
>
> **AESOP**

Bugging the customer

When my customers get really busy and stop responding to my faxes and phone calls, I use a little humor to get their attention. I stamp a Bugs Bunny figure on my usual letterhead and fax the page over to the customer. My clients almost invariably call back asking what happened to the rest of my fax, or they realize I want to know "What's up, Doc?" and call me explaining why they haven't been in touch. I always respond by telling them that when all else fails, I have to resort to "bugging" them for their own good!

Diana Mashini, Manager

> **"A jest often decides matters of importance more effectually and happily than seriousness."**
>
> **HORACE**

Lifetime guarantee

To reassure our customers that their satisfaction is our top priority,

we offer them a written no-time-limit guarantee – and stand behind it.

The guarantee also shows customers that we know our work will stand

the test of time. We tell our customers, "If it's not right, we make it

right – now – no ifs, ands or buts."

Jule Pels, Builder

"There's no great mystery to satisfying your customer. Build them a quality product and treat them with respect. It's that simple."

LEE IACOCCA

You word it well

My company deals almost exclusively with engineering personnel from large manufacturing firms. We try to distribute our technical data to as many of these engineers as possible, so we always ask our current contact for a list of other engineers to whom we can send our literature. At one time the question elicited little or no response – then we changed the way we asked. With our old method, current contacts didn't see how giving the names away would benefit their friends. Now we ask, "Is there anyone else there who might benefit from having our technical catalog on hand?" Because this question shows our interest in offering a benefit to our contact's associates, we now get a much better response when we ask for referrals.

Randy Cordes, Sales and Marketing Manager

> **"It is the man determines what is said, not the words."**
>
> **HENRY DAVID THOREAU**

Cash in on cover sheets

Gaining a competitive edge means taking advantage of every opportunity to raise interest in what my company does and what we sell. For an effective (and very inexpensive!) way to spread the word about new products or services, special sales and events and other happenings, we use fax cover pages to advertise them. These cover pages grab the recipient's attention more than other businesses' cover pages and, best of all, every fax we send gives us a chance to set an appointment or make a sale.

Terry Grady, Director of Sales and Marketing

> **"If you want to succeed in the world, you must make your own opportunities."**
>
> **JOHN B. GOUGH**

After-hours prospecting pays off

During the early stages of my selling career, I often put myself in the company owner's shoes and asked myself what I'd have to do to make the company successful. For starters, I knew I needed to build my customer base but I was limiting my prospecting time to 9-to-5 business hours. After a few months I began getting to work early, leaving late and coming in on Saturdays. I quickly discovered that my prospecting efforts paid off even more during off-hours than during regular working hours. I reached the decision maker more often and my success helped me build a larger customer base and lay the foundation for a successful sales career.

Stan Alie, Account Executive

Put your money where your mouth is

I came up with a unique and effective method to help me close a diffi-

cult deal with a client who insists my price is too high. I rip a $50 bill

in half and hand half of it to my client, telling him that if he can find

a better value for his money, I'll give him the other half. Many of my

clients assume that I'd have to be pretty confident to rip a $50 bill in

half, so this strategy makes it easier to get the order

quickly instead of waiting for prospects to look for a

lower price.

Cheryl Amantea, Sales Professional

> **"What costs nothing is worth nothing."**
>
> **ANONYMOUS**

The salesperson's new clothes

My father is an old sales pro and the source of many creative selling solutions. One of his best is a fun motivational idea we call "Clothes The Sale." It started 12 years ago when we had an all-male sales team. Today we have updated it to include all 60 salespeople, about 10 of whom are women. Every year each salesperson in our company submits personal monthly sales goals for the coming year. Each month, those who achieve their goals win an article of clothing that makes up a suit – for example, first-time goal achievers always win top-quality underwear, then for each monthly goal thereafter the winner gets socks, shoes, shirt, pants, belt, tie, jacket, etc. At the year-end sales meeting and party, the entire sales crew must appear onstage in however many (or few) clothes they won that year. Participation in the program is completely voluntary. Instead of selecting the clothing, we give each participant vouchers for top-quality clothing at the store of their choice. We find that we have 99 percent participation in the program each year because it turns into such a fun way for everyone to

compete on a level playing field for sales goals.

Jeff Colvin, Vice President

> **"Clothes and manners do not make the man;
> but, when he is made,
> they greatly improve his appearance."**
>
> **HENRY WARD BEECHER**

And thanks to all

I have taken the process of writing thank-you notes to all who purchase ads in our publication a step further than most by requiring our sales staff to send thank yous at every stage of our sales process – to all prospects when they request information, to all prospects who become clients, and even to those prospects who decide not to take advantage of our services. This accomplishes two things. Psychologically, our salespeople are able to handle the rejection of a no much better by ending with an upbeat thank you for the time the prospect invested considering our fine service. Second, we leave the prospect with a top-notch professional impression. I have even had prospects change their mind after initially saying no to our service, as the result of a brief thank-you note. This works especially well if the prospect was questioning our integrity, yet never voiced it as an objection.

Darron Richardson, Regional Director

A fair question

Salespeople often have to ask questions that make their prospects feel

like they're being interrogated, making them react by getting defen-

sive or clamming up. To soften the blow of a difficult question, precede

it by saying, "Is it a fair question to ask you...?" This technique helps

keep clients from feeling threatened or irritated, so

they feel more at ease opening up to you.

Christopher O. Jackson,
National Sales Manager

> **"Questions show
> the mind's range,
> and answers it's
> subtlety."**
>
> **JOSEPH JOUBERT**

When you're smiling

When I was first hired as a sales representative at Clayton Homes, my boss told me that the first thing I needed to do was find a way to encourage my prospects and customers to respond to me individually. I went down to the local bookstore and bought smiley face stickers, which I now use on my name tag, business cards and all correspon-

> **"A smile is a light in the window of a face which shows that the heart is home."**
> UNKNOWN

dence. Now my prospects have a way to remember my smiling face, and anything that helps them remember me can't possibly hurt my sales. It's something to smile about!

Renita Durall, Sales Representative

Upselling by design

As the owner of a desktop publishing firm, I find out my customers' budget so I can create an attractive design they can afford. Usually, they ask for an economical black-and-white design on colored paper. Once I find out what they want to spend, I create two designs: one in black and white that falls well within their price range, and one in full color that exceeds their budget by 35 percent. Many clients are so impressed with the color design that they choose it over the less costly black and white – and increase the size of their order! Show prospects you respect their budget needs by designing a proposal within their price range, but don't miss out on the chance to make a bigger sale by designing another proposal (and explaining its advantages) that exceeds their budget limit. Your customers might end up spending more than you – or they – thought they would!

Angela Batchelor, Creative Consultant/Owner

Chocolate triumph

As a television advertising salesperson, I've found that sports programming is very popular with my buyers. As each sports season approaches, I order chocolate basketballs, footballs, golf balls or other sports-related items from my chocolate maker. I use the candy to put a smile on my prospect's face before my presentation, and to thank them after they've bought. Best of all, you can adapt the idea to almost any industry. Team up with a small chocolatier who can offer customized service and has a variety of molds on hand. Almost everyone loves chocolate, and even if some of your prospects don't, the gesture may be enough to help you get the sale anyway.

Donna Batdorff, Sales Professional

> **"Any month whose name contains the letter a, e or u is the proper time for chocolate."**
>
> **SANDRA BOYNTON**

Ring-a-ding

I had been trying to reach the true decision maker at an ad agency for weeks. At first when I got his answering machine I just hung up. Then when I kept on getting his machine, I started leaving my name, phone number and a brief message as to why I was calling. This went on for about a month with absolutely no personal contact. I was very frustrated until I had a brainstorm. I started to leave a message with my name, phone number and a brief message then, while I was still on the line, I stopped and started talking to myself out loud, saying, "Idiot, no wonder he hasn't called back. This person is really a machine and machines can't call back." Then I hung up. Five minutes later he called back saying he wasn't a machine. We both laughed a little and I got a face-to-face appointment.

Barry Katz, Sales Professional

> **"The soul may be a mere pretense,
> the mind makes very little sense.
> So let us value the appeal
> of that which we can taste and feel."**
>
> **PIET HEIN**

The right touch

Research by Dr. J. Hornik at the University of Chicago showed that a light, brief (1/2 second) touch on the upper arm of shoppers caused them to shop 63 percent longer and spend 23 percent more than people who had not been touched. Dr. Hornik also found that timing was important. Touch someone shortly before you want that person to do something – agree to another appointment, buy something, etc. Although touch has magic, it should not replace the handshake but be an added way to express warmth and a friendly desire to help.

John A. Quatrini, Sales Professional

What it's not

Many times when making cold calls to an executive at work, I encounter a secretary or assistant who wants to know who I am, what I want, etc. The assistant does not mean to be difficult but is doing a good job of protecting the manager's time. I have found that the best way past this screening process starts with maintaining a firm attitude in your voice and then basically saying what the call is not about. For example: If I'm calling an attorney's office and am asked what the call is in reference to, I respond by saying that it is not about a pending case. Ninety percent of the time I get right through. I use the same type of process with other professionals and find it works almost all the time.

Marvin S. Goldman, Sales Professional

> **"Do not reveal your thoughts to everyone, lest you drive away your good luck."**
>
> **APOCRYPHA**

The blocker

This tip may seem simple, but when you have perfected it with the correct nuance, tone and pitch, your success rate at getting through a prospect's screener can climb from 10 or 20 percent to a whopping 70 or 80 percent. Mine did! Here's how it works.

Screener: *ABC Systems, may I help you?*

Salesperson: *Good morning. Is Mr. Smith in?*

Screener: *I'll check. May I say who is calling?*

Salesperson: *Yes. This is Joe Sales. Who's this?*

Screener: *Oh, uh, Wendy.*

Salesperson: *Hello, Wendy, is he in?*

Screener: *Just a moment.*

This method establishes reciprocity with the receptionist at the first line of defense and, once established, it almost always works.

John T. Raisin, Sales Professional

Don't sell price

When I was asked to bid on a printing job for a local TV station, I made a proposal, and at a second meeting, the general manager told me they were still waiting for more bids. When I followed up by phone, the printed forms buyer told me my prices were lower than one company's but higher than the other. At two more meetings with the forms buyer and the station manager I was able to convince them to buy from me, although my prices were still 10 percent higher than the next lowest bidder. How? I pointed out the benefits of buying from a regional supplier rather than an out-of-state supplier. I pointed out the experience and knowledge of our family-run business and all that implies in quality control and personalized service. I banked on the personal relationship I had developed with the station manager. I was persistent but patient over a period of five months. I sold quality, convenience, service and peace of mind. I made a $30,000 sale because of my feature/benefit mindset.

Anup Gupta, Sales Professional

The gator letter

I hate it when prospects don't return my calls. Because I don't want to be a pain in the neck to prospects, I have developed what I call my "alligator letter." It begins: "Surely you must be so busy that the alligators have turned and eaten you alive." Then it goes on with a series of check-off squares and these lines:

☐ "I'm swamped. Call me after the first of _____ (month) so we can talk."

☐ "Don't call me. I'll call you."

☐ "Please take us off your list."

☐ "As soon as I get through this project, we can talk."

This letter goes out with a self-addressed, stamped envelope so all the prospect has to do is drop it in the mail to me. I have used this quite successfully and my prospects seem to enjoy it. Often they apologize for not returning my calls and explain that they just didn't have an answer for me at the time.

Roz Eaves, Sales Professional

Keep a goin'

Remember that persistence is not pressure. It is a release from pressure. It eliminates fear, inhibition, doubt and excuses. It creates freedom, builds success and opens doors to satisfaction. So, don't give up when a prospect says no. Continue to listen, question, learn and close. Your customers will thank you for it and you'll be greasing the persistence wheel for many more circles of success.

Roy Bernius, Sales Professional

"I am not the smartest or the most talented person in the world, but I succeeded because I keep going and going and going."

SYLVESTER STALLONE

The customer comes first

A few years ago I was in the market for a new car. I knew what I wanted and what I planned to pay. I decided to telephone a few dealerships

> **"The opportunity that God sends does not wake him up who is asleep."**
>
> **SENEGALESE PROVERB**

to see what they would offer. Although I called several dealers, to my dismay the switchboard operator told me, "I'm sorry, all the salesmen are in a sales meeting." I was about to give up when I reached the last dealership on my list, where the switchboard operator said, "I'm sorry, all the salesmen are in a sales meeting, but if you'll hold, I'll call one out for you." Guess who got my business. Talk among yourselves at your next sales meeting. I've given you the topic.

Brad R. Lathrop, Sales Professional

> "Man's rise or fall, success or failure, happiness or unhappiness depends on his attitude...a man's attitude will create the situation he imagines."
>
> JAMES LANE ALLEN

Business is booming!

Our company actively works with its employees to help them understand that people like to do business with successful companies. To that end, when prospects or customers ask, "How's business?" we have been trained to respond with an upbeat and positive phrase. We say things like "It's terrific and we appreciate your business" or "We're getting bigger and better with every order." Remember, perception is nine-tenths of success so if you want to be a winner, start sounding like one. And by the way, how's business?

John Knutson, Sales Professional

Get to know me

I have just learned the most important sales lesson – get to know your customers' problems. A local carpet dealer had committed to a regular ad schedule with my newspaper to coincide with a large display in our local mall. At the last minute he called and canceled the ads. Since I did not want to lose the business I called and asked what was the problem.

> **"The great pleasure of ignorance is the pleasure of asking questions."**
>
> **ROBERT LYND**

It turned out he needed a phone to do the mall display and the mall could not provide him with a hookup. I called one of my other accounts – a cellular phone company – arranged for a dealer demo for the duration of the show and, bingo, I was in business again. The carpet dealer bought the phone, the cellular dealer was happy and I kept both accounts. But nothing would have worked out if I hadn't asked about my customer's problem.

Dawn Rowe, Sales Professional

A real smoker

I've seen a lot of salespeople burn out because of the high level of stress created by the way they handle rejection. Many of them seem to turn to smoking to let off steam after a rejection. I submit that there are better ways to handle the stress inherent in selling than filling your lungs with smoke. Along with your sales magazines and technical journals, subscribe to a magazine on outdoor activities or nature. If you can get outside and back into nature, whether it's a lakeside picnic at a city park or a hike up Mount Washington, you will find that concentrating on the beauty around you is the antithesis of the stress of selling, and you will immediately feel that stress drain out of your body and mind. I try to get out for a 10-mile hike at least once a month. Remember, it's much healthier to spend your money on hiking boots than cigarettes.

Allen Hefner, Systems Consultant

> **"Father Time is not always a hard parent,
> and, though he tarries for none of his
> children, often lays his hand lightly on those
> who have used him well."**
>
> **CHARLES DICKENS**

Please wait

Years ago when I began my selling career, one customer used to keep

me cooling my heels in the lobby for 45 to 60 minutes before every

call. During the actual sales meeting, however, he was always conge-

nial and friendly. Although I would ask him if there was a better time

to call on him, he would just say that no time was better than any

other. So I was condemned to wait in the lobby before each call. After

a year of this I finally figured out a way to use this lobby time to my

best advantage. I'd sit down in the lobby, take out my paperwork and

begin on the current day's work. I wrote call reports and follow-up let-

ters, studied product literature and reviewed what I wanted to sell to this account. Then during the second year of calling on this account, the wait became shorter, the customer and I began having lunch together, and, over the next three to four years, the customer and I really got to know each other. At this point he told me the reason why he made salespeople wait in the lobby. He said that most of them were not prepared for the call and asked him what they should sell him. His own sales force was highly trained and motivated and he expected the same from salespeople who called on him. Today this account is in our top 10 and the customer has become a good friend who calls me to set appointments. My advice about customers who make you wait is this: Find a good use for your valuable time and don't waste it getting aggravated. Be ready to serve and you may just find real value in waiting in the lobby.

Daryl A. Allen, President

Read the want ads for leads

Many salespeople read newspapers as a source of leads by reading announcements of promotions and news stories. I also find a good source of leads in the help wanted pages. For instance, many companies will explain in their ads the expansion plans or growth that have prompted the new position. In addition, when I see an ad run by a prospect or former customer for the job position I call on, i.e., Human Resource Director, I file that ad away for 60 days – 30 days for the company to fill the position, 30 days for the new person to start in the job – and then I call. Often I am the first person calling them when they are ready to make some buying decisions. I have penetrated many accounts by using this prospecting technique.

> **"A good newspaper is a nation talking to itself."**
>
> **ARTHUR MILLER**

Dona Blunt, President

Set the agenda

Once you have an appointment with the buyer and you know the number of topics you need to discuss is extensive, fax an agenda that thanks the buyer for granting the appointment and briefly details the various points you wish to discuss during your meeting. This agenda serves two purposes. First, it confirms your appointment and further cements it in the buyer's datebook. Second, it provides the buyer the opportunity to prepare for your call. Amazingly, it will often lead to the buyer allotting more time for your call simply because the agenda has been set.

> **"Plans get you into things but you got to work your way out."**
>
> **WILL ROGERS**

Thomas J. Wilson, Key Accounts Manager

Still selling the sizzle

As a 21-year-old struggling with my first sales job vending wholesale paper and janitorial supplies, I wasn't having much success. I kept trodding on from door to door, but the orders just weren't coming in.

Elmer Wheeler's book *Sell the Sizzle and Not the Steak* taught me to sell "sparkling" sanitary toilets instead of bowl cleaner, and "wet-looking" floors instead of floor wax. And wow – did the orders start rolling in! Find the magic phrase for your product or service and watch your sales take off.

Steve Webb, Sales Professional

> **"You can stroke people with words."**
>
> F. SCOTT FITZGERALD

Laid an egg lately?

When one of my best clients stopped returning my calls, I decided to appeal to his sense of humor! I contracted with a local agency to have a singing telegram delivered to the client's office by an actor costumed as a large yellow chicken. I personalized my message to the tune of "Happy Days Are Here Again" and left the rest up to the chicken! Early the next morning, a chagrined but laughing client called to say I had definitely captured his attention in a very creative manner! The chicken got me an appointment and restored our pleasant client/sales rep relationship. After several months, people are still talking about the day the chicken came to call. Never underestimate what a touch of humor can do for your sales!

Carol Gordon, Executive Director

Free advertising!

An effective voice mail greeting can help you outshine your competition. Instead of using a run-of-the-mill greeting, I take the opportunity to sell my service. My current message says, "Hello, this is Paramount Cleaning Services where we dry clean your carpet with the HOST Dry Extraction Carpet Cleaning System. HOST is recommended or approved by more than 100 carpet and fiber manufacturers worldwide, and was top rated by *Consumer Reports* magazine. We're sorry we can't take your call in person, but would love the opportunity to serve you. So please leave your name, telephone number and a brief message after the tone, and we'll return your call as soon as possible. Thank you." This message fits on a 30-second incoming greeting tape and doubles as a 30-second commercial. Many callers like to comparison shop by phone, but sharing interesting information via voice mail helps pique their interest and put your business at the top of their list.

Robert Ford, President

Mirror, mirror

I work for an online service and do 100 percent telephone sales. I have found that having a mirror in front of me and observing myself as I speak with customers by phone helps me sell. Without the mirror I often found myself doing other things and allowing my focus and concentration to stray from the sale and the customer, lowering my closing rate. With the mirror, I not only imagine myself in front of the prospect, but watch myself as if I actually were. This self-observation disciplines me to stay focused on my call and increases my confidence in myself, which in turn increases my sales.

Ginger Cole, Telemarketing Sales Representative

> **"Almost always it is the fear of being ourselves that brings us to the mirror."**
>
> **ANTONIO PORCHIA**

Hot cold call strategy

I sell a new product line to independent merchants. Invariably, the objections to carrying the product are the same – price, cash flow, shelf space and timing – even though store owners indicate the product is clever and well made. When I make a sales call I have learned not to begin with the product and the value it adds. Instead, I first stroll through the store like a customer and assess the bandwidth of the product lines, high and low prices and broadly estimate the annual revenue streams. Then I introduce myself to the owner, manager or decision maker. I indicate that I am scouting for stores that would be appropriate to carry a new product line and that I don't want to take up their time if their marketing strategies and objectives are different from ours. This gets the client talking and opens them up to probing questions. Frequently, I can tell that there are no clear strategies or objectives. I then summarize or formalize the key marketing strategy and objectives in a way that highlights the value of my product: "So what I understand is that you are primarily targeting such and such a customer and plan to move about X pieces per month year-round with a top price of Y and a Z percent markup. Is that in the ballpark?" This paves the way for a product presentation. Now I can personalize by referencing the store prices of other merchandise to illustrate the value of my product, how it fits into the present marketing mix and how it will promote the sale of other items.

Joel Fullmer, Sales Professional

"There is always a best way of doing everything, if it be to boil an egg."

RALPH WALDO EMERSON

Start out strong

In our office, we have found a cold calling technique that is not only consistent with our soft-sell approach, but also puts the customer at ease immediately. As soon as the salesperson has given their introduction and formal greeting, they ask the customer, "Have I caught you at a good time?" This accomplishes one of two things: The customer is disarmed because he/she feels that the salesperson is empathetic and respectful of their time (making the customer more apt to listen and buy) or the salesperson can plan for follow-up at a later time so neither party's time is wasted. From the onset of the sales call, the key is to be proactive rather than reactive in your approach. The result is stronger rapport and less rejection.

Anne Richardson, Assistant Sales Manager

"All doors open to courtesy."

THOMAS FULLER

I just called to say "How are you?"

Developing a long-term relationship with an account requires more than just quality products and superior service. To encourage a lasting, profitable relationship I always strive to learn more about my customers on a strictly personal level. With this in mind, I have found it tremendously effective to ensure that at least every third phone call to each of my accounts is not business related, but simply a call to see how the "person" – not the account – is doing. Encourage your customers to talk about their families, hobbies and activities outside the office. Even the busiest buyer welcomes this brief social call and we both enjoy discovering each other's outside interests. As a secondary benefit, a much greater percentage of my first phone calls are accepted, virtually eliminating unnecessary "phone tag."

John Alofs, President/Owner

Pause and effect

I couldn't understand why one of my prospects wouldn't place an order with me – until I stopped talking long enough to let him make a decision. On my first call on this buyer, I extolled the virtues of my floor tile and its potential benefits to him while he listened attentively, but I left empty-handed and confused as to where I was going wrong. When I

> **"One never repents of having spoken too little, but often of having spoken too much."**
>
> PHILLIPE DE COMMYNES

returned a month later I adopted a new approach, presented the basic product benefits, then kept quiet as the buyer and I stared at each other. This truly was a pregnant pause, because when the buyer finally spoke it was to place the largest order I had ever received. Apparently, my incessant talking on the first call had interfered with his ability to make a buying decision. Try giving your prospects a moment to think after you've made your presentation. A conversational pause isn't always negative – it could be pregnant with potential.

Thomas B. Porter, Sales Professional

The power of three

There is a simple rule I use when preparing sales presentations for my

customers: Always limit the presentation to three reasons for buying

the product or service. This helps focus the interview on the most crit-

ical ways I can be of service. The three reasons in each specific pre-

sentation will vary – much as customers' needs vary. I keep a list of

10 to 15 potential benefits that prospects might

realize from my product or service. From that list, I

pick the three reasons most likely to be relevant to

my prospective client. The other handful of benefits

is now ammunition for answering objections that

may arise during the sales process. Using this

approach will give clarity to your presentations and

> **"The ability to simplify means to eliminate the unnecessary so that the necessary may speak."**
>
> **HANS HOFMANN**
>
>

will virtually eliminate rambling sales presentations that are a waste

of time for all parties involved.

Tom Trinko, Regional Manager

Don't do as someone else does

Many years ago when I was an absolute beginner in the sales profession I was employed for the summer by my brother, who was an outstanding salesman in the ladies' apparel industry. My job was to chauffeur him to his various accounts and carry his samples to the room where he would meet "the buyer." On one sales call, he was really hot and writing a terrific order when he showed the buyer the last dress in his line. The buyer said, "That is the ugliest dress I have ever seen," whereupon my brother pulled the dress off its hanger, rolled it into a ball and tossed it over the edge of the buyer's desk and into the corner. The buyer looked in astonishment and asked Bill why he had done that. His response was, "I greatly respect your taste and if that is your opinion of that item, I shall seriously consider taking it out of my line." As we left the buyer, my brother told me to make haste back to our motel where he quickly steamed the wrinkles out of the dress. We continued to show that item to the rest of his accounts and prospects.

When I actually entered the job market, my brother got me a job working for his company in a different territory. One night prior to an important sales call the next morning, I called Bill and asked him for some advice so I could start making some sales. He said, "Look, brother, you have traveled with me and have seen me sell, just imitate what I have done." The next day, as I was nervously showing my line of ladies' dresses, the buyer complained about the appearance of one of the items. I immediately balled up the dress and tossed it into the corner. Unfortunately for me there was a styrofoam cup of coffee in the path of the toss. It spilled all over the buyer's desk and I was promptly ushered out with no order. The moral is, don't try to completely imitate another's style, but pick and choose until you are comfortable with your own presentation and what works for you.

Lawrence A. Malin, National Sales Manager

It never hurts to ask

MarketSmart produces semi-custom promotional newsletters and postcards for retail flower shops, greenhouses and garden centers throughout the country. We respond to requests for literature by sending a comprehensive literature packet containing a cover letter, samples of our work, explanatory information on how the programs work, pricing and ordering information and a copy of our newsletter. When I call each prospect to make certain they've received the material I jump right in with a non-threatening icebreaker certain to engage them in dialogue: "So did you like it? Hate it? What did you think?" When prospects realize that I'm more interested in hearing what they have to say than in making a sales pitch, they usually start talking. Even if they tell me that they're still months away from making a purchase, they always tell me what they really think. As a result, both of us benefit from a productive conversation, and I get important feedback from prospects on a daily basis.

Cathy Cain, Sales Professional

The price of quality

Sooner or later almost every salesperson will hear those five little words: "Your prices are too high!" One effective response convinces prospects to admit that high quality often costs a little more. When I hear the all-too-familiar price objection I respond with, "Our prices are too high compared to what?" Asking that question in a serious, calm manner (without sounding or getting defensive) makes your prospects think about what they've said. If you sell to a business that prides itself on its quality products and prices their products accordingly, point that out. On a sales call to a fine restaurateur, compliment the buyer on a specific dish and say, "For the price you charge for that item, I am sure you use quality ingredients that warrant that price – right? What we offer (mention your product's attributes and how the prospect benefits) also warrants this price." This technique is applicable to most businesses and may change the way your prospects think about your product and price.

Lynn Potts, Sales Professional

A new use for the microwave

Humidity is high most of the year in Louisiana, and it's almost impossible to print multiple pages of the second side of a two-sided page in my laser printer due to the paper crinkling up. I tried to store our paper so that it would be protected from the humidity, but could find no dehumidifying cabinet to hold our office paper reams. After enduring months of crinkled copy after crinkled copy, I tried microwaving the paper to reduce the excess moisture. I left the outside paper wrapper open to let the steam escape and it worked. For the first time in months I could get 50 double-sided copies through my laser printer in a crinkle-free single pass. Even the print quality seems to have improved.

Mark McBride, Sales Professional

> **"Even when I was young I suspected that much might be done in a better way."**
>
> **HENRY FORD, SR.**

Elevator advertising

The next time you find yourself alone in an elevator, take advantage of free advertising. Take out a business card and print this message on the back: "Sue, please call this great sales rep and place an order! M." Be sure to sign with a first initial other than your own. Place the business card, note side up, on the floor under the elevator floor buttons. The card will stand out like a neon sign to any decision makers who get on after you.

James Mosvick, Sales Professional

> **"There is no such thing as bad publicity except your own obituary."**
>
> **BRENDAN BEHAN**
>
>

> "The best product must be sold. People won't come to you and take it away from you. You must go to them."
>
> **EDNA NEWMAN**

900 reasons to switch

I had been trying for three years to convince a heating and air conditioning service to switch to my pager company. I knew I could provide better service at a lower cost than the service they had been using, but I couldn't seem to convince them to give me a try. I finally got their attention by writing a personal check to the company for $900, which is about how much they could save with my pager company in three years' time. Of course I printed VOID across the check, but my creative approach got my point across and the next week one of the owners called me to switch companies. After three years, they're still with me.

John Schram, Sales Professional

A newsworthy practice

To (unobtrusively) keep my company in front of customers and prospects, I produce a company newsletter that educates my customers and prospects on issues that will improve their business performance. The one-page, general interest newsletter familiarizes readers with my products and services. At the same time, it also helps build my reputation by positioning my company and staff as industry experts. Instead of spending hour after hour calling on prospective clients, I add new prospects to the newsletter mailing list. I've gotten terrific feedback from clients and prospects alike who enjoy learning more about our industry, and who appreciate my efforts to help them make better buying decisions by clearly explaining what I have to offer. When clients pass my newsletter around as lunchtime reading material, I'm confident in the knowledge that I'm providing a needed service.

Jennifer Triplett, Sales Professional

Research and (profit) development

The small training and consulting firm I work for needed to boost response to its direct mail campaign. We found the solution in going the extra mile for our customers. During information seminars, we often received dozens of questions but simply didn't have time to address all of them. Instead of leaving the questions unanswered, I took time after the seminars to research each question and send the person who asked it a personal letter along with articles and reference material supporting my answer. Over 50 percent of those who received the letters became long-term clients – about 10 times our usual success rate! It took a lot of time and effort to conduct the research and write the responses, but the results were well worth it.

Rick Craig, Sales Professional

Follow up with flair

I use a personalized postcard for marketing and follow up that leaves a lasting impression on my prospects. My postcards match my business card in style and appearance and feature my photo and slogan on the front. They're perfect for thank-you notes, short letters or announcements and reminders of my services or upcoming events. In a business world that gets less and less personal by the day, my postcard's personal touch helps keep my business relationships warm and friendly.

Joeann Fossland, President

> **"From a man's face, I can read his character..."**
>
> **PETRONIUS**

I've got your number

When I got tired of time-consuming searches for phone numbers jotted down on scraps of paper, thumbing through database printouts for numbers or calling information, I used my word processor and laser printer to create a list of my accounts' main telephone numbers sized to fit a 3 x 5-inch space, cut it out and had it laminated at a local copy center. Now I've got a personal phone directory that gives me access to the numbers I call most in a fraction of the time it takes to flip through an address book or call 411. Both sides of the paper give me room for about 70 numbers for customers, airlines and car rental agencies (including club membership numbers), other members of my sales team and general information numbers for my company that customers often ask for. The card also eliminates the need to carry more than a dozen hotel and airline membership cards and creates a great list of accounts and contacts I can mentally review for action items. I also created a credit-card-size version for my wallet with airline, hotel, family and emergency numbers like my insurance company,

doctor and bank. For the cost of about $1 I have a convenient way to

keep my important numbers at my fingertips.

John Kristoff, Sales Professional

"It is best to do things systematically, since we are only human, and disorder is our worst enemy."

HESIOD

Prospecting en route

I've found a great way to prospect smarter instead of harder. I always carry a clipboard in my car with a notepad and pen. Every time I drive to work or to an appointment I pick up a huge number of leads just by looking out the window. Here's what I recommend: The next time you're stopped at a traffic light, keep your eyes peeled for leads on the sides of delivery trucks, trailer sidewalls, billboards, building facades, lawns or construction sites. Take notice of changes in your marketplace – a newly vacant parking lot or a once-empty lot now filled with cars. Get acquainted with mail carriers, next-day delivery people and real estate agents who can keep you in the know as to who's doing what that might be of professional interest to you. You might find yourself spending less time and effort prospecting, but increasing your prospects and profits.

Leonard G. Blumenschine III, Sales Representative

Thanks to the gatekeeper

When people ask me the secret of my eight-year sales success, I always answer, "Intense follow-up." Lots of salespeople send a follow-up thank-you note to their prospects, but I take the time to send a personal note to the often-overlooked receptionist or gatekeeper as well. The note comes as a pleasant surprise to many of them and sets me apart from my competitors. Best of all, it helps break down barriers and, on my next visit, I usually get a warm welcome from the receptionist.

John Supplesa, Sales Representative

> **"Gratitude is the most exquisite form of courtesy."**
>
> **JACQUES MARITAIN**

Get your closing probability

The next time your prospect asks for time to think over a buying decision, say, "Mr. Prospect, that would be fine. I understand your desire to think it over. But let me ask you this – when I call you back next week, what is the probability, in percentage terms, that you and I will be doing business?" This question requires prospects to give you an idea of whether or not they'll buy. If they say it's unlikely that they will, you can ask questions to find out why not and salvage the sale.

Rick Passaro, Sales Professional

> **"Nothing is more difficult, and therefore more precious, than to be able to decide."**
>
> **NAPOLEON**

Information worth saving

Occasionally, I will call on a client who is interested in my company's services, but does not have an immediate need. The prospect will usually say, "Send me something for my files for future reference." Rather than view this as the kiss of death or badger the prospects for more specific dates, which they usually don't know, I give them exactly what they ask for: our company's brochures and references – in a bright red hanging file folder. The folder is clearly marked on the view-tab with my company's name and primary service area. This way, the client does not have to think about whether it is worth creating a file for my literature – I have already given them the information in a ready-to-use format. When I call back I find that they still have my materials where they need them the most – at their fingertips!

Gretchen Sauerman, Sales Professional

Ask the experts

Twice a year, we hold training seminars for our 20 managers covering seven states. For at least one of those seminars we invite several industry representatives to sit on a guest panel of experts and answer our sales managers' questions. For two to three hours, these experts talk about what turns them off on sales calls, what new products they'd like to see that our company doesn't provide or anything else our sales managers want to know more about. These question-and-answer sessions have provided a wealth of valuable information and resulted in many new product innovations and improvements.

Traci Esch, Marketing Associate

"Learn as though you would never be able to master it, hold it as though you would be in fear of losing it."

CONFUCIUS

Telephone premium

Clyde Records had sold 348,000 people a record by comedian/musician Ray Stevens. With such a large customer base, they called on an Akron, Ohio, company for help in using the list in other ways. The expert's suggestion? "We developed a program that offered a set of two brand-new Ray Stevens videos, selling for $39.95. As an incentive, buyers were given a third Stevens video (a Ray Stevens TV pilot featuring various guest stars) as a premium. We told prospects they could keep the premium whether or not they bought the two-video set. We knew that some of these people would have already seen or bought the free video so we suggested that they give it to a friend as a gift and keep the two-video set for themselves." With a response rate of 14 percent, much higher than expected through direct mail, Clyde Records converted a substantial number of one-time buyers into repeat customers.

Steve Pittendrigh, Sales Professional

Follow-up flag

I learned early in my sales career that follow up is an essential part of the selling cycle. I was a sales representative for the Better Business Bureau of Houston selling BBB memberships when I called on a fairly new oil change business. I went through my presentation and the customer told me that he would really like to be a member. First, however, he had to put a flagpole outside his business. He was a Vietnam vet and the flagpole was first on his list of things to do. I told him that I would contact him again when I saw his flagpole installed. I passed by his location weekly for a full eight months until, finally, I saw the flagpole go up. I immediately called him and reminded him of our agreement. The next day I picked up his membership application check. It may have been a long wait, but the follow-up call did pay off.

Debra Beasley, Sales Professional

> **"Everything comes if a man will only wait."**
>
> **BENJAMIN DISRAELI**

Storm troops

Brainstorming is a great but often underused business tool. In a networking group I belong to, we frequently brainstorm on such topics as marketing techniques, time management and self-motivation. The group includes salespeople, a CPA, a dental lab owner, a newspaper publisher, a financial planner and an astrologer. They all have different ideas that others can adapt. Sometimes an idea is new to a member, sometimes it's an old idea with a

> **"An invasion of armies can be resisted, but not an idea whose time has come."**
>
> **VICTOR HUGO**
>
>

new adaptation. I take the brainstorming idea one step further and use it with clients. We brainstorm about marketing plans and where to find and reach new markets. Drawing off of the ideas of others is a great way to multiply your brain power and your profits.

Christine Moses, Sales Professional

> **"To do two things at once is to do neither."**
>
> PUBLILIUS SYRUS

Business development time

When surgeons are in surgery, they are not returning phone calls, getting beeped, filling out paperwork, interviewing or doing anything else but operating. Similarly, I have found that salespeople need to treat their business development time as if it were their own version of sales surgery. I have developed something for my sales team called business development days. Once a week, we designate an entire day as business development day, during which one activity, and one activity alone, is undertaken: building new business. This means that there is no work on contracts, no meetings, no paperwork to fill out, no customer service issues to attend to, no anything other than calling for appointments and identifying and qualifying new business opportunities. In support of them, I pledge to protect the sales team from external "intrusions" into business development time. The day starts with a continental breakfast for everyone. At 9:00, everyone spends 30 seconds describing which list or which leads they intend to prospect for the day. At 9:15, the bell sounds and we're off to the races. We hold contests wherein everyone who contacts a certain number of prospects wins a prize (free lunch, a gift certificate, etc.). In another contest, everyone who confirms a certain number of appointments wins another prize. At the end of the day, we all get together to recap individual performances and award prizes. As important as it is for the salesperson to have uninterrupted time to conduct surgery ("build the business"), it is equally symbolic to declare that members of my sales team are indeed sales professionals and will religiously perform the most important piece of their respective responsibility, building new business. Business development days have filled both of these needs for me.

Robert N. West, Director Of Sales

The referral two-step

I have a little different perspective on getting referrals. It involves two stages. The first stage – trust – involves building integrity, friendship and confidence between you and your customer. Before you can actually ask for a referral, you must become a trusted supplier to your customer. The second level – sharing – involves asking the customer to share his good fortune and good experience with you as a supplier. Once you have passed the first level, the second should be almost automatic. But don't be too proud to ask.

John Seib, Sales Professional

> **"Trust men and they will be true to you..."**
>
> **RALPH WALDO EMERSON**

A little respect

To make my prospects respect an appointment we've made, I send out a letter confirming the appointment date. I enclose a couple of small, self-adhesive labels with my name and phone number and a place to write in the date and time of the appointment. I suggest that the prospect place the stickers on their planning calendar. As a result, I have far fewer missed appointments, and when prospects do break an appointment, they usually call me in advance and offer to reschedule.

Steven Donovan, Sales Representative

> **"Who breaks his faith no faith is held with him."**
>
> **SEIGNEUR DU BARTAS**

Prospect all day long

I keep a notebook handy in my car to jot down the names and addresses of businesses I pass that look like they could use my product. I vary my routes as often as possible and have asked my customer service representative to do the same thing. It's a great way to develop new prospect files all the time.

Debbie Shames, Sales Professional

"How many opportunities present themselves to a man without his noticing them?"

ARABIC PROVERB

That's why I'm calling

Over the years I have brought literally hundreds of customers on board by using one simple phrase. I use it on the initial call to set up an appointment. If the prospect says, "We already have a service," I say, "Well, that's why I'm calling." If the prospect says, "I'm happy with my current supplier," I say, "That's why I'm calling." If the prospect says, "We don't use a service. We do that ourselves," I say, "Yes, that's why I'm calling." This is a great way to set the prospect back for just a moment to give you time to speak your piece. I have seen many a perplexed prospect who thought he had just shot me out of the saddle do a second take when I came back with "That is just why I am calling."

Gordon Hoover, Vice President

Thanks...for nothing

Send your customer a thank-you note for not getting the order. Why?

Many companies are required to get bids from different companies.

Sometimes these bids require many calls and lots of number crunching and, since you didn't get the business the first time, the buyer may feel bad calling you to "spin your wheels" again when a new project arises. Your note will remove any strain and show you are a professional who doesn't bear a grudge. Here's how your thank-you note should go: "Thanks for letting us bid (make a presentation). I'm sorry that we couldn't help you this time. Please keep us in mind for future projects and feel free to call or fax me for jobs in the future." Such a thank-you note leaves the door open for bids and sales opportunities in the future. I learned this technique many years ago from Tom Hopkins – it works!

Alan H. Goldstein, Vice President

Eye contact

You can tell how your presentation is going simply by watching your prospect's eyes. If they dart around the room, check paperwork, or gaze out the window, it's time to shift gears. Say something unexpected or introduce a new idea, but do something different. Ask prospects what's on their mind and why you lost their attention. You might even want to cut the meeting short and offer to come back another time.

Dane Hooper, Sales Professional

> **"The eyes have one language everywhere."**
>
> **GEORGE HERBERT**

Good morning

When you absolutely have to get an appointment but a prospect won't see you, try this. For four consecutive weeks, deliver a "good morning" breakfast in attractive gift bags with sales literature and a note on corporate stationery. Week 1: Bagels and a note that says, "Please enjoy your breakfast with my compliments while you read my most current sales literature. I'll be in touch." Week 2: Croissants and a small jar of jam plus a note that says, "Please enjoy your breakfast and, when you are in a jam, call on us." Week 3: Rolls and a note that says, "(Your company's name) keeps your business rolling." Week 4: Small loaf of bread with a note that says, "(Your company name) will 'rise' to any occasion. Call when you 'knead' us." During weeks one, two and three simply leave the breakfast with the receptionist or the prospect's assistant. On the last week, ask to see the prospect to deliver the breakfast personally. Be prepared to make a presentation.

Jennifer Jankowski, Account Representative

> **"The reason why we have two ears and only one mouth is that we may listen the more and talk the less."**
>
> **ZENO OF CITIUM**

Can we talk?

Over the years, I've learned that successful selling depends on your ability to listen. It's crucial to let your prospects talk about themselves and their business. A good rule to follow is: Talk 20 percent of the time, and spend the remaining 80 percent listening. My appointment-to-close ratio has increased dramatically since I made this change.

Justin A. Horn, Sales Professional

At least 10 ways

I provide prospects with at least 10 ways to use the product I sell. To compile my list, I call customers who currently use my product and ask how they use it. Once I have this master list, I tailor it to the needs of each new prospect. I learn all I can about the company I am calling on and cross-reference its needs with my list. For example, if health care clinicians are using a textbook as a reference in the clinic, I can sell the same textbook to professors by recommending they use it as a reference in the university library. As I compile my list, I learn from customers and they feel flattered that I ask them to share their thoughts. This generates goodwill and future sales.

Diana M. Martin, Marketing

> **"Pleasing ware is half sold."**
> **GEORGE HERBERT**

Listen up!

I sell advertising for a major national magazine. Like many salespeople I tend to talk more than I listen. But I'm working on it after one experience in my territory. I decided to call on the president of a small manufacturing company, hoping he would be able to set aside some time to discuss marketing his products via my publication. When he took the call I was surprised that he agreed to a meeting with no hesitation. In our first meeting he told me that he never gives anyone business until they have made at least 10 calls on him. Well, I made the 10 calls in a very short period of time and, when advertising budgets were allocated, we got the lion's share of this company's pot. Are you listening?

Denise Lovat, Sales Professional

> **"Give every man thine ear, but few thy voice."**
>
> **SHAKESPEARE**

Speak your customer's language

When I know my customers have been using my competitors' products and are used to their item numbers and product names, I know that this "language barrier" sometimes prevents me from getting the sale. Since my customers don't have the time or motivation to learn another manufacturer's nomenclature and item numbers, I make it easy for them. In the margin of my price list I added a column and use it to place our competitor's item numbers next to my company's equivalent products. This tactic helps my customers understand just what they're getting for their money and how my products compare (favorably) to what they already have. My customers have told me that this was the best thing I've done to earn more of their business!

Bill Cullen, Executive Marketing Representative

Call back later

Often a prospect will show interest in my product but will ask me to call back at a later time to go over details. Then when I call again, the prospect is often out of the office or busy. When this happens and I get the sense that this prospect is important and also very busy, I send an inexpensive gift – a small bouquet if the prospect is a female, a coffee cup arrangement if it is a male – with a note saying: "I realize you are busy. I think my services would help alleviate some of your problems." This gesture usually elicits a thank-you call and then I make the appointment.

Phillip D. Alcantar, Chief Marketing Officer

> **"You can accomplish by kindness what you cannot do by force."**
>
> **PUBLILIUS SYRUS**

May I quote you on that?

Your customers' praise is often the most effective advertising you can get. As I was returning to my lunch table during a break at one of my recent seminars, I overheard a participant exclaim, "Gary's tapes doubled our sales!" In response I immediately asked her, "Can I quote you on that?" She agreed, and I picked up a valuable new testimonial for my mailing piece. To get more testimonials from your happy customers, give some of your long-time clients a call and ask them what they think of your product or why they've remained so loyal to your company. Be prepared with open-ended questions to get close-lipped customers to tell you how they use your product, and use the information to help close future customers. Not only does "quote mining" supply you with valuable testimonials, it also helps reinforce your customers' decisions to buy and encourages them to continue to do so.

Dr. Gary Goodman, President

> "Of cheerfulness, or good temper, the more it
> is spent, the more of it remains."
>
> **RALPH WALDO EMERSON**

A cheerful good day

I am a sales manager for a small manufacturing company. For a short time, I also held the position of purchasing manager at the same time. In doing both jobs simultaneously, I discovered a little tip that I have passed down to my sales and customer service employees. When speaking with customers, always have a bright and cheery voice. Always use the customer's name and make sure they hang up with the feeling that you enjoyed speaking with them. This may be something everyone knows, but does everyone make an effort to give this to every phone call? We have found it very effective.

Lynne M. Taylor, Sales Manager

TIP #86

(Virtually) foolproof referrals

My favorite technique for getting referrals helps build rapport with the customers who give them to me. If my demonstration gets stalled or I'm waiting to talk to the decision maker, I always ask the support people, "Where did you work before you came here?" They usually worked in a similar industry doing a similar job, so their previous employer often has the same needs as my current prospect. When one person I asked told me where he'd worked before, I'd never heard of the company, but he said he thought they needed my product. He was right. The call I made to the company brought me my largest order yet. What better way to find out about qualified prospects?

Nancy Colligan, Sales Representative

> **"Foolish are the generals who ignore the daily information from the trenches."**
>
> **ANONYMOUS**

An easier introduction

When making sales calls door-to-door, I always make sure I'm holding

my computer and/or briefcase in my left hand, so my

right is free to shake my prospect's hand. I can make

a more professional impression if I'm not fumbling

with whatever I'm carrying and can shake hands

easily. Also, instead of facing the door, I stand side-

> **"I hate the giving of the hand unless the whole man accompanies it."**
>
> **RALPH WALDO EMERSON**

ways so my prospects can get a look at me before I see them and I

don't look as though I'm peering into their homes ready to pounce on

them. The more I can do to put my prospects at ease, the more likely

they are to listen and perhaps buy.

Claude Peltz, CLU, ChFC

Don't be shy

When prospects call our company and don't leave a message, that leaves us no chance to earn their business. Now our voice mail message tells them what's in it for them when they leave a message. Our automated greeting promises a $5.00 gift certificate to any caller who doesn't receive a call back within two hours. At first we thought $5.00 wouldn't convince people to leave a message when they didn't want to, but we've found that our callers often time us and are disappointed when we call before our time's up. Our voice mail system tells us when the call was placed so we know when to start timing ourselves, and after responding to around 8,000 phone calls, we've only had to give out three gift certificates. When customers forget to leave their numbers, we just save the message until they call back and ask for their certificate. With this idea, we get a chance to turn all our callers into customers.

Kevin Swark, General Manager

Promise in writing

To show we're committed to great service, at the beginning of each year my account executives give their customers a list of the 10 services they personally guarantee to perform for them (i.e., returning phone calls on the same day). This lets customers know exactly what kind of service they can expect, and invites them to complain when the salesperson doesn't meet those expectations.

Vincent Capozzi,
Director of Municipal Business

> **"To oblige persons often costs little and helps much."**
>
> **BALTASAR GRACIAN**

Pages of success

This motivational sales tool has lasting impact on my sales team and generates positive publicity for our company. We award salespeople a new book for their sales library for every testimonial letter they receive. With this reward, the salesperson wins with a valuable testimonial to show prospects how happy other customers are with our product. Plus, we circulate these testimonials throughout the company and present the books to the salespeople at a sales meeting, so they get recognition for a job well done. The company benefits by keeping a master book of testimonial letters to help when we solicit a national account. What's more, this program educates our salespeople (they're more eager to read books they've won) while it motivates them.

Linda P. Kester, Sales Professional

> **"Books give not wisdom where was none before, / But where some is, there reading makes it more."**
>
> **SIR JOHN HARINGTON**

> **"Flowers and plants are silent presences,
> they nourish every sense except the ear."**
>
> **MAY SARTON**

Sales in bloom

About five years ago, we came up with a sincere, warm (but not too personal) way to show our customers we appreciate them. Each spring we design a flyer that includes a poem and thank-you sentiment drawing parallels between the rebirth of nature and the renewing of friendship and success. We then add the flyer to a packet of hardy flower seeds. Everyone seems to appreciate the sentiment, and one client even gave us a bouquet grown from the seeds we gave her.

Mary Anne Hogue, President

Recruiting more sales

Customer understanding is critical to making the sale, but finding out about a prospect isn't always easy. In addition to the usual product literature and annual report, I've found that a company's college recruitment brochure often tells me a lot about it. Designed to "sell" students on a company, these brochures frequently feature names and photos of division heads, including new hires, and provide such information as challenges and mission statements of individual departments that you often can't find in other sources. To get a brochure, call the prospect company's personnel department as if you were a potential job applicant or parent job hunting for your son or daughter. The information you find might be your link to a sale.

> **"Knowledge is of two kinds. We know a subject ourselves, or we know where we can find information upon it."**
>
> **SAMUEL JOHNSON**

Anne Miller, Sales Professional

Multiple-choice objection

When I hear "I want to think it over," instead of drilling my prospects,

I put them at ease by saying, "You know, Ms. Prospect, when someone tells me they want to think about their decision, it usually means (a) they feel the price is too high or value is too low, (b) they don't believe in my company, my product or me, (c) they're afraid of making a mistake, (d) they sense the product may be more troublesome than the problem, (e)

> **"The aim of argument, or of discussion, should not be victory, but progress."**
>
> **JOSEPH JOUBERT**

they think the product will soon be obsolete or (f) there's some other

reason why they're not making a decision. Would you share which cat-

egory you fall under?" This approach usually convinces my prospects

to open up, so I can help them without interrogating them.

Carlos Llarena, Director of Recruitment

Free distribution

To promote a new product (in our case, a new book) and get our catalog out to qualified prospects, we wrote to a target group of existing customers, promising them a free copy of the book if they'd send us a self-mailer postcard requesting at least five of our mail-order catalogs to pass around to colleagues. Many of these customers ended up showing the book and catalog to an average of 10 other people, so we got a lot of good exposure and quickly sold many copies of the new book and of "backlist" titles from the catalog. Of course, we also made quite a few new customers in the process.

Carey Giudici, Sales Manager

"The excellence in a gift lies in its appropriateness rather than its value."

CHARLES DUDLEY WARNER

Paying for attention

I often know my prospects need my products, but getting an audience with them long enough to show them can be tough. When I encounter prospects who are unwilling to speak with me, I make them an offer they can't refuse. First I ask them what their time is worth. Then, I ask them to meet with me and tell them that if, at the end of the call, they don't feel they've benefited, I'll reimburse them for their time. In return, I get a commitment from them to buy from me if I'm able to meet their needs, and to provide referrals if they know of anyone else who can use my product. This tactic requires a great deal of faith in one's product and one's ability to sell it, but it can help you get the few minutes you need to convince your prospect to buy.

Donald J. Engels Jr., CLU

> **"Our costliest expenditure is time."**
>
> **THEOPHRASTUS**

Sweet-talking salespeople

When my car rental agents acted more like they were taking a census than making a sale, I had to find out how to make them slow down and warm up when asking customers to upgrade or buy extras. To solve the problem, I told them to treat their customers as if they were a friend's elderly grandmother who'd come to visit. Instead of asking, "Are you coming in or staying outside?" now they say, "Would you like to come in and sit down and visit a while?" Instead of "Do you take the coverages?" they explain, "Our Loss Damage Waiver protects the car with no deductible in case it is wrecked, stolen or damaged. It's a great plan that we highly recommend. Would you like to take it?" This kinder, gentler way of talking makes the prospect feel special and sweetens up our sales as well.

Don Pennington, Revenue Sales Manager

Sales by mail

My partner and I specialize in collectible dolls, so to boost sales we
decided to create a free newsletter for collectors. Each issue includes
current information on the dolls, special events and
information on retired dolls. We run inexpensive ads
in our local newspaper classified section under
"Antiques and Collectibles," and advertise in other
state newspapers. In each ad we offer the free
newsletter. To each new prospect who responds we
send the most recent edition of the newsletter plus a
welcome letter, three business cards to pass on to other collectors and
a "sign up a friend" form. The newsletter helps position us as experts
in the field, and as response to our ads grows, so do our sales.

Traci Warrington, Partner

> **"Advertising
> helps raise the
> standard of living
> by raising the
> standard of
> longing."**
>
> **UNKNOWN**

Cold call thaw

To reduce cold call jitters and increase my odds of getting an appointment, I fax my prospect a short, personalized letter introducing myself, my company and my product and stating that I will call in a few days to follow up. A day or two later, I call in the early morning or late evening when I'm sure the prospect won't be in. I leave a message stating that I'm calling as promised to confirm that the prospect received my fax, then I briefly summarize the initial letter and say I'll call again. This message gets my name in front of the prospect a second time before the final step: another phone call placed when I hope to find him or her at work. By this time the prospect has seen my name at least once, so I'm no longer a stranger. I explain that I'm calling again to confirm that the prospect got my fax, and to see if I can set up a time to meet. I'm more comfortable when I first speak to them knowing that I've already provided the general introductory information.

Lain Chroust Ehmann, Associate

> **"The lowest of jewelry thieves is the robber of that precious jewel of another's time."**
>
> **ADLAI STEVENSON**

An eggsellent idea

If you've got a one-minute egg timer, you've got a good way to get your prospect's attention and, possibly, an appointment. Mail the egg timer to your prospect with a note requesting one minute of their time. Should you get the appointment, bring along another egg timer and set it for one minute to show that you're sincere and that you value your prospect's time. Chances are, your prospect won't stop you after 60 seconds and your fun, creative approach will help you make a sale.

Kristi Gacke, Regional Director of Sales

Special bulletin

To announce the coming of our salespeople to their customers' territories, I send out an amusing personal newswire to all of our customers. Simply titled "Debbie's Newswire," it includes funny clip art like a picture of a TV with the caption "Turn us on!" or an image of the sun over the words "Hot Stuff." I also include amusing facts about each salesperson, and a "truth or dare" section in which the truth is new product info and the dare is a challenge for customers to call their salesperson to find out more. These newswires often prompt customer calls to our office, and the salespeople report a great response from on the road.

Debbie Kelley, Marketing Coordinator

> **"Total absence of humor renders life impossible."**
>
> **COLETTE**

Business breakfast

To save valuable working hours and cut down on expenses, I encourage my salespeople to conduct business over breakfast rather than lunch or dinner. The meal is just as pleasant, but costs a lot less and takes less time away from peak selling hours. It also ensures my salespeople have eaten the most important meal of the day, so they're energized and ready to be productive.

Paul Fedors, Director

> **"One cannot think well, love well, sleep well, if one has not dined well."**
>
> **VIRGINIA WOOLF**

Worth a thousand sales

When it's not enough to tell prospects what a terrific job you do, show them. I make my points with a three-ring binder full of 8" x 10" photos of some of my company's past projects. When we finish with a project, we arrange a follow-up call with the customer, at which time we take photos of the job to add to the book. This special attention makes our customers feel the job we did for them is truly outstanding, and helps us get the referrals that make up 15 percent of our business. Of course, the photos help to enhance and expand what is already a terrific sales tool.

Frank Karycinski, Sales Professional

> **"Things seen are mightier than things heard."**
>
> **ALFRED, LORD TENNYSON**

Money talks

To make a lasting impression on prospects at a large business expo my company (and our competitors) planned to attend, I wanted to offer a memorable giveaway item. I wanted something more original than mugs or key rings, but I had to stay within my budget. My solution was as close as my wallet. I found a supplier of oddly shaped, clear plastic ziplock baggies and placed a dollar bill in each one. On the outside of each bag I affixed a label that read, "Our CPAs put more money in your pocket." This item was such a hit that the local press took pictures that gave my company extra exposure and I got phone calls for weeks from people who loved my idea and had since used it themselves.

Terri Sommella, Marketing Director

> **"Ready money is Aladdin's lamp."**
>
> **GEORGE GORDON, LORD BYRON**

> **"Ours is the country where, in order to sell your product, you don't so much point out its merits as you first work like hell to sell yourself."**
>
> LOUIS KRONENBERGER

Welcome wagon

With so many executives and companies moving to the growing city where I live, I appointed myself head of the welcoming committee. When I learn that my prospect is new to the state, I call the state tourist office and request that an information packet be mailed directly to their business. Then I follow up with a letter welcoming the prospect to the area. This friendly gesture helps get my prospects acquainted with their new surroundings and makes their relocation a little easier. Of course it also helps me make a memorable first impression that gives me an edge on the competition.

Kristen Quintero, Training Consultant

Something for nothing

When you know your product's the best on the market, sometimes you can convince your prospects more easily by giving them a free sample. When we go to trade shows, we give away samples of our cleaning products instead of other promo items. No matter what your industry, beating your competition often means proving to your customers that your product is superior. At my company, the samples we distribute allow us to put our money where our mouth is and do just that.

Lisa Corona, Sales & Marketing

> ## "Presents, believe me, seduce both men and gods."
> **OVID**

TIP #106

Butter up your buyers

The products I sell are in no way related to popcorn, but this popular snack has earned me the nickname of "popcorn man" among my customers. When I want to show my appreciation to prospects, customers or helpful receptionists, I say it with popcorn. The microwavable packets are inexpensive, easy to carry and distribute, and don't go stale. Best of all, this idea sets me apart from my competitors and lets my valued customers know that when they need me, I'm ready to POP in on a moment's notice!

Bob Hill, Director of Marketing

> **"That's something I've noticed about food: Whenever there's a crisis if you can get people to eating normally things get better."**
>
> **MADELEINE L'ENGLE**

> **"Why is it that you can sometimes feel
> the reality of people more keenly through a
> letter than face to face?"**
>
> **ANNE MORROW LINDBERGH**

Second-look letters

Businesspeople are so inundated with junk mail these days that we know we have to make our letters stand out to make sure they get opened. We use a regular postage stamp on our prospecting letters, and often enclose such small gifts as pens or memo pads with the company name and phone number. The outside of the envelope (which may be an unusual size and/or color) often features graphics with funny or timely messages. We can't get our message across unless the customer reads what's inside the envelope, so we try to make the outside as appealing as possible.

Angela Vosler, Investment Representative

Don't overlook the log

Whenever I call on a customer, I never fail to check the visitors' log that's usually found at the reception desk. One glance often tells me who my competitors are, who they're calling on and when. When I sign in, I give away as little information as possible, using a department name instead of my name and substituting my company acronym for its full name. Many of the prospects I get from the log are already qualified, and I recently received a large order from information I found there.

Scott Pitney, Sales Manager

"The competitor to be feared is one who never bothers about you at all, but goes on making his own business better all the time."

HENRY FORD, SR.

Open for business

Six years ago, my family founded a consulting firm focusing on records management and personnel services. To give our associates an inside look at our business, every year we hold an open house. Guests help themselves to international cuisine while they tour our offices, view demonstrations of current information management software and pick up brochures and business cards. A guest book helps us keep track of attendees and attendance. These yearly get-togethers are terrific networking opportunities and are a fun and easy way to increase business while projecting a positive image to our customers.

Tina Merwin, Office Manager

> **"A guest never forgets the host who had treated him kindly."**
>
> **HOMER**

The optimum 15

As a financial consultant for a large bank, I advise clients where to

best place their CDs, annuities, mutual funds, etc. Bank personnel

> **"Better three hours too soon than a minute too late."**
>
> **SHAKESPEARE**
>
>

refer many of their customers to me and I then call

them to schedule an appointment. I was recently

given a new idea at a seminar, which has proven to

be successful. In speaking with potential clients to

set up an appointment, schedule the appointment at

15 minutes before or 15 minutes after the hour. I

have found that people show up on time (and sometimes early) and I

have very few no shows.

Wendy Wallis, Sales Vice President

The doctor is in

The pharmaceutical company I represent allows me to be very creative in my efforts to attract more customers. Knowing that some of my "impossible-to-see" prospects (female physicians of dermatology) were prescribing a competitive product, I decided to stage a "Ladies' Dr. Derm Night" – an elegant, classy cocktail/dinner event. The event brought all my prospects together to exchange opinions and ideas, and I brought in a well-known speaker to talk about some new therapies for diseases (along with the benefits of my products). Out of the 31 female dermatologists in my territory, 26 attended, and every one of them asked me if I would organize another event in the future. In my business, a two- to three-point increase in market share for the year is the goal, but I was able to boost sales in my territory by two points in just two months. Now, I get hugs from those dermatologists I was once never able to see!

Debbie Preston, Sales Professional

Moving toward a sale

It's getting harder and harder to stand out from all the other sales-people vying for your buyer's attention, so a little creativity often goes a long way toward helping differentiate you from everyone else. Once I've spoken with my prospect and piqued their interest in my products,

> **"It's all right to hesitate if you then go ahead."**
>
> **BERTOLT BRECHT**

I send them our package of information. Since it can be tough to reach them again by phone, I send a fax, and in the space for messages on the cover sheet, I print a graphic of a moving truck or an 18-wheeler and on the body of the truck I type, "It's your move." This idea often gives my buyer a laugh, and gives me many callbacks that I might not have gotten otherwise.

Shelley Naser, Telecenter Manager

A matter of trust

Your customers won't know they can trust you until

you prove to them that you always live up to your com-

mitments and deliver what you promise. To make sure

I get off on the right foot with my customers, I often

intentionally withhold my business card after my initial call on them,

but promise to send the prospect a business card when I return to the

office. As soon as I get back to my office, I write up a quick thank-you

note, enclose the business card as promised and promptly mail it off to

my customer. When you do this, your customer will be reminded of the

commitment you made to mail it and they'll see that you kept your

word. You might still have a long way to go before you get the sale, but

earning your buyer's trust is a great start.

John F. Kirchner, Manager of Sales and Customer Service

> **"To be trusted is a greater compliment than to be loved."**
>
> **GEORGE MACDONALD**

Sales à la carte

Whenever we're holding a sales meeting, expecting a client to come into the office or planning some other sales function, I fax a copy of our local deli's lunch specials of the day along with an agenda for the meeting or event. When the salespeople and/or customers arrive, they're usually very grateful that I planned ahead for lunch, which helps me build rapport with them and promotes an atmosphere of motivating goodwill for that day's function – and I share the credit for the sales or improved productivity that result. Finding out what's for lunch can help build teamwork in a whole new way!

Patricia Pollak, Sales Professional

> **"There is nothing to which men, while they have food and drink, cannot reconcile themselves."**
>
> **GEORGE SANTAYANA**

Too much information

If you wouldn't consider giving the same canned presentation to all your prospects, be sure to customize the information you send them as well. Because prospects often just want to know what they'll have to pay and what they'll get out of your product, think twice before sending them long case studies, statistics or other highly detailed info they don't want or need. Instead, save their time by providing several specific monthly payment options, then briefly recapping what they get in return: "For less than $1,000 a month we

> **"Information's pretty thin stuff, unless mixed with experience."**
>
> **CLARENCE DAY**
>
>

can provide your organization with a product that will protect you from losses that would more than triple this monthly expense if you didn't have this protection." This gives your prospect realistic, concrete figures to show them that your product is a wise investment.

Mike Reis, Senior Technical Assistant

Pushing the hot buttons

At trade shows we try to establish a personal and memorable connection with visitors by giving every prospect who stops at our booth a large, attractive button with ribbons emblazoned with our company logo or a product we're trying to promote. We tell the prospect that if they continue to wear the button around the trade show grounds they can win a prize if one of our company representatives spots them and takes their picture. After our employee takes a picture of each person he sees wearing a button, he has the prospect write his name and phone number on the back of the picture. At the end of the day, we put all the pictures in a box and draw winners. We end up with a lot of free advertising from show attendees wearing our buttons all day, and taking the pictures helps raise onlookers' interest in visiting our booth. Finally, our company benefits from a much more significant trade show presence and leaves a lasting positive impression on our prospects.

Steve McCain, Sales Professional

Would the real objection please come forward?

When customers say they want to "think over" their buying decision,

it's often safe to assume that they have an objection they're not shar-

ing. Asking "What do you want to think over?" can seem

pushy and intimidating, which probably won't help you

uncover the real problem. Instead, ask, "Is it a question

of price?" then quietly wait for a response. By guessing

a specific objection, you'll encourage prospects to cor-

rect you by stating their true concern. If your sugges-

> **"Thinking is the most unhealthy thing in the world."**
>
> **OSCAR WILDE**
>
>

tion is correct, you probably found out what's really making your buyer

hesitate. You might be surprised at how much this strategy improves

your closing ratio.

Micky Huet, President

Earth-friendly attention getter

Despite all the effort you might put into writing them, many cover letters are never read by the people who receive them. To save time and paper and make my cover letters stand out, mine consist of only two or three powerful sentences neatly handwritten or typed on a quarter of a sheet of paper. I made a rubber stamp reading, "Please accept my personalized note, I like to recycle," and use it to stamp each of my letters in an upper corner. This method immediately resulted in more calls for me. I'm convinced that my letters are read more often because of it and that it helps my prospects remember me.

Kari Koivuniemi, Sales Professional

> "Promise is most given when the least is said."
>
> **GEORGE CHAPMAN**

Call me back – or else

You can reach a prospect's voice mail, but you can't make him call back. Of course, you can boost your chances of a return call with a message that's anything but run of the mill. If my prospect doesn't call me back after several messages, I make a joke out of my determination to get through by saying, "Joe, you're not ignoring me are you? You know you can run but you cannot hide." Or I'll use a humorous threat: "I'm afraid that I'm going to have to sing my next message to you if I don't hear back from you and believe me, it's not pretty." My funny messages almost always get me a return call, but if they don't I make good on my "threat." Only a few of my prospects have been immune to my singing!

Lisa Schrader, Business Development Manager

> **"Men will let you abuse them if only you will make them laugh."**
>
> **HENRY WARD BEECHER**

TIP #120

Your big day

Whenever follow up involves a historical date that is important to the client, I use a milestone software printout. Milestone software is mostly shareware (evaluation copies are available at many shareware distribution sites on the Web), but I use registered versions of "News of the Past," "On this Day" and "The Birthday Chronicle," plus the commercial version of "Birthday Newsletters" by Expert. Milestone software collates important events, birthdays of famous people and popular songs of the day, together with an idea about the cost of living at the time of the client's anniversary or birthdate. My clients are overwhelmed by the attention to their special day. I even use milestone software now to break the ice with prospects who have their wedding anniversaries printed in the newspaper. Does it work? How many other insurance men do you know who get messages of thanks in their voice mail or thank-you cards from grateful prospects for their marketing pieces? It beats cold calling.

Tony Brezovski, Insurance Agent

Casual day every day

I used to go out every day and "beat the bushes" for new customers in my suit and tie, but as the current trend in corporate America seems to be dressing down, with "casual Fridays" on the rise, I decided to jump on the bandwagon. Knowing how important it is to keep my name and my company's in front of my buyers, I went shopping for casual clothing, then had my name and my company's tastefully embroidered on it. My customers don't have to worry about remembering my name, so they can focus on my presentation more, and the clothing promotes a more casual atmosphere that helps put my buyers at ease. My sales are up, many of my fellow salespeople have followed my lead and now more of my customers know me by name.

Jeff Burr, National Sales Manager

> **"Know, first, who you are, then adorn yourself accordingly."**
>
> **EPICTETUS**

Door-to-door, floor-to-floor

As an authorized sales agent for Britt Business Systems, which sells

Xerox copiers and fax equipment, I'm required to make 100 cold calls

each month. Hearing prospects say "no" to my face can be demotivat-

> **"I will go any-where provided it is forward."**
>
> **DAVID LIVINGSTONE**

ing, so I needed a way to keep me moving toward my

cold call quota so I can reach it on time. With this

method I can make up to 30 cold calls in one-and-a-half

hours: I choose a building that's likely to be filled with

qualified prospects, then start at the top floor and

work my way down floor by floor, using the stairs so I don't waste time

waiting for elevators. On each floor, I start at one end of the hall, then

work my way back to the stairwell. By the time I'm finished I've called

on every office in the building. While most salespeople are working to

reach the top, I'm working to reach the bottom!

Erika Vogel, Account Executive

Quiz master

If you're a telemarketer you probably talk to voice mail 10 times more than you speak with a live person. I've found being creative when leaving messages on voice mail is very effective. For example, keep trivia questions next to the phone. Next time you get a voice mail start your message by asking a trivia question on a related industry and ask them to call back for the answer to the trivia question and the answer to their (insert industry) needs. The answer will be industry specific. You'll be surprised with the response you get. Test a variety of techniques. See which ones potential customers respond to bests.

Cathy Steiner, Advertising Sales Professional

> **"To question a
> wise man is the
> beginning of
> wisdom."**
>
> **GERMAN PROVERB**

Power Tools For Success

Promote professionalism in selling throughout your company. The editors of *Selling Power* have created a series of easy-to-use power tools to enhance your knowledge, expand your skills and help you in your quest to be the best.

① Selling Power Magazine

In every issue of *Selling Power*, you'll find money-making ideas from leading sales experts who help you close more sales with less stress. Plus, you'll stay up-to-the-minute on the latest trends in selling, sales management and sales automation while keeping your motivation at peak level. In just a few minutes of reading you'll get the selling ammunition you need to:
• get more profitable leads
• overcome price resistance
• become the master of your time
• get the "silent prospect" to open up
• increase your ability to manage

• develop new closing techniques and more...

A one-year subscription will pay for itself many times over in new sales and higher commissions.
▶ $33 per year for 9 issues. (Low corporate rates also available)

② Selling Power's Best

A powerful collection of action-oriented essays. In his latest book, *Selling Power* publisher Gerhard Gschwandtner offers a powerful collection of his best editorials, covering such vital sales subjects as overcoming disappointment, what leadership means, how to manage your attitude, what your customers really expect, how to achieve balance,

how to plan for more success, how to harness the power of ideas.

Order *Selling Power's Best* for a motivational lift, for sound selling advice and to help increase your productivity.
▶ Hardcover. Only $19.95, quantity discounts available.

③ The Sales Script Book

This is a collection of the most powerful and useful phrases (scripts) a sales professional can use to counter any objection and close any sale.

The Sales Script Book contains 420 tested responses to 30 of the most important and most difficult customer objections. If your customer

says, "I want to think it over," you simply open up tab divider #21 and you'll find 17 tested responses. If the customer says, "Your price is too high," you simply flip to tab #4 and find 23 tested sentences to handle price objections. Put 420 of the most awesome lines at your fingertips to add thousands of dollars to your sales.
▶ (8 1/2" x 11", 3-ring binder) Only $99

④ The Sales Closing Book

This is a limited edition handbook that contains an exclusive collection of more than 270 tested sales closes that can skyrocket your sales and your income. These powerful closes have been proven and tested by the top sales achievers in the U.S. and overseas. In many cases, these closes have been responsible for securing orders in excess of one million dollars.

Here is just a brief sample of what you can expect to find in this book:
• 15 objection closes that work every time
• 41 tested price closes to close price buyers with confidence
• 6 superb story closes that apply to any selling situation
• 25 powerful negotiation closes and many more techniques to help you earn more money

Ideal for telemarketing, sales training and anyone who wants to win more customers.
▶ (8 1/2" x 11", 3-ring binder) Only $99

⑤ The Sales Question Book

This well-organized, tab-indexed sales tool is packed with the greatest sales questions to get more productive answers from every customer. In minutes you can select powerful questions to structure

your sales call from opening to close.
• 101 of the best questions to build rapport
• 59 tested questions for handling objections
• 43 of the most productive upselling questions
• 169 powerful closing questions and much more

Stay in control of every sales call with 1,100 tested selling questions at your fingertips. This book is ideal for writing sales scripts and it's a great resource for training salespeople. A vital working tool for any sales office.
▶ (8 1/2" x 11", 3-ring binder) Only $99

⑥ Superachievers

Now you can benefit from the hard-earned lessons of the likes of Ronald Reagan, Zig Ziglar, Mary Kay Ash, Dr. Norman Vincent Peale, Dr. Ken Cooper and many more. All of the 12 superachievers profiled in this best-

selling book have been featured on the cover of *Selling Power*. Each chapter offers a five-point action plan so you, too, can develop your individual blueprint for success.

This special self-help book is for sales leaders who have come to realize that by changing your heroes, you can change the direction of your life.

▶ Hardcover. Not sold in bookstores. Only $19, quantity discounts available.

⑦ The Sales Manager's Problem Solver

This is a practical, fill-in-the-blanks sales management tool designed to help your salespeople boost sales knowledge, sharpen skills and increase motivation.

How does it work? It's a simple, six-step process: (1) You evaluate your salespeople's current performance. (2) You measure the gaps. (3) You develop an improvement plan.

(4) You coach your salespeople. (5) You measure the results. (6) You reward the achievement.

The Sales Manager's Problem Solver is a tested system to guide your salespeople on the road to ongoing improvement. It will help you become part of the solution to any of your salespeople's problems.

▶ Only $17.95

⑧ Thoughts To Sell By

Here is the perfect motivational reminder. *Selling Power*'s latest book is an easy-to-use reference guide for good thoughts and wise proverbs. It's designed for the busy sales professional who is looking at the bright side of life, even when the world appears to be drowning in negativity. Put it in your shirt pocket and instantly turn waiting time into quality time.

One hundred unique

quotes, tastefully illustrated and carefully selected for today's sales professional. An ideal gift idea for every person on your sales force.

▶ Only $5.95

⑨ The Eagle: America's Inspiration

This exciting new book from the publishers of *Selling Power* magazine combines dramatic action photography of the Bald Eagle in its natural habitat with inspirational quotes and fascinating facts about this powerful bird. Each chapter showcases the eagle's characteristics by drawing parallels to noble and desirable human qualities.

The amazing action photographs were supplied by Jack Barrie, North America's foremost photographer of Bald Eagles. During the past 15 years, Barrie has taken over 20,000 pictures of Bald

Eagles in Alaska, the Pacific Northwest, and Canada.

His photographs have appeared in countless magazines, books, ads and motivational posters.

▶ Only $29.95, quantity discounts available.

The Eagle Poster: Power

This poster has been printed with great care. Each poster is laminated to ensure a smooth, wrinkle-free and water-repellent surface. Benefit from the memorable and meaningful quote. Use it as a subtle, visual reminder to stretch your abilities.

Power: *Reach high, for stars lie hidden in your soul. Dream deep, for every dream*

precedes the goal. Pamela Vaull Starr *(other eagle posters available)*

▶ Only $25

⑩ *The Funnel Poster*

Make your next sales meeting more productive with the Funnel Strategy Poster. A perfect power tool for teaching your salespeople how to manage their client base more profitably. Use this educational poster as a daily reminder for your salespeople to replenish their prospect base, shorten their sales cycle and capture higher quality prospects. Includes five wallet-size cards for quick review. An inexpensive way to improve sales meetings and increase sales. Get one

for every sales office today. (11" x 24")

▶ Only $10

⑪ *Sales Training Posters*

While most salespeople ad lib their responses to customer objections, trained professionals can deliver three, four or more responses in a heartbeat. How do they do it? Simple – they have a *Selling Power* training poster right in their office. When a customer brings up an objection, they glance at the poster, smile and read off the best response. (18" x 24")

▶ Your price is too high: $10.

▶ I have to think it over: $10.

To order :

Complete the coupon on pg. 144 then choose one of the following ordering methods: **Call** TOLL FREE 1-800-752-7355 In VA call 540/752-7000 **Fax** order 540/752-7001 **Mail** to Selling Power, P.O. Box 5467, Fredericksburg, VA 22403 Look for Selling Power on **the Web** at HTTP://WWW.SELLINGPOWER.COM